I0166968

Maria's Wonderland

Written by
Amber Hawthorne-Spratlen

Illustrated by
Bonnie Lemaire

Halo
PUBLISHING
INTERNATIONAL

Copyright © 2022 Amber Hawthorne-Spratlen
Illustrated by Bonnie Lemaire
All rights reserved.

No part of this book may be reproduced in any manner
whatsoever without the prior written permission of the publisher,
except in the case of brief quotations embodied in reviews.

ISBN: 978-1-63765-265-7
LCCN: 2022912214

Halo
PUBLISHING
INTERNATIONAL

Halo Publishing International, LLC
www.halopublishing.com

Printed and bound in the United States of America

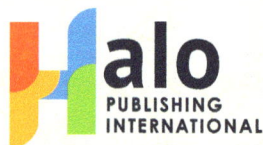

This book is dedicated to all of the students for whom I have had the pleasure of facilitating their early years of learning. I was blessed to be your teacher, yet you have all taught me invaluable life lessons!

Maria, Maria, do you hear me talking to you?

4

I can hear you. I know where I am, and I know my name.

Why do the grown-ups keep asking me this?

Hmm...I wonder why.

Maria, Maria

Well, my name is Maria, and I am five years old.

Mrs. Scarvelli is my teacher. She, and basically EVERY grown-up, thinks I don't understand what they are saying.

Hmm...I wonder why.

I am fully aware of what's going on… but everyone is so LOUD!

Similar to the honking horn of the car that just drove past, I hear Mrs. Scarvelli moving papers, and Lindsay keeps sneezing!

Hmm…I wonder why.

There's a humming noise coming from somewhere. Jackson keeps screaming and crying, and the light in the classroom keeps flashing.

There's really too much going on!!!!

There's ALWAYS too much going on.

Hmm...I wonder why.

When I try to talk, I look at the person speaking to me...like, I really watch their mouth.

But I hear other things around me, and... now, I am focused on those noises!

Hmm...I wonder why.

Who can tell me what shape this is?

14

I can talk, I really can, but I can't do a lot of things at the same time.

I can talk. I know that I can talk. I have heard myself speak. I promise!

But now I have to press this button to speak because nobody can hear me.

Hmm...I wonder why.

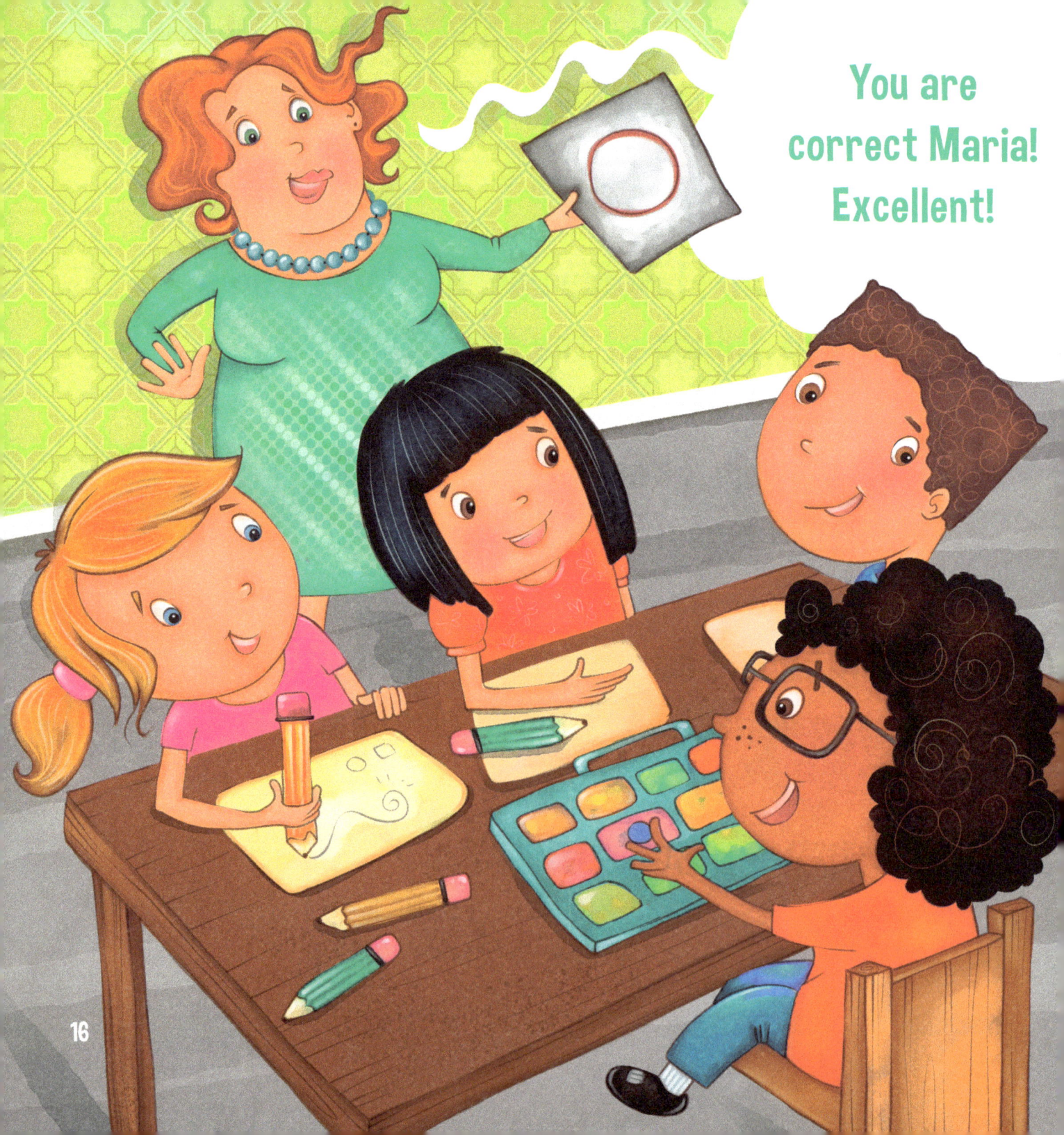

It's a circle!!!! It's a circle!!!!

I know it is.

I found the circle button on my new machine. I pressed it, and a voice came out if it and said, "It is a circle."

Mrs. Scarvelli told me that she is proud of me and that I can continue to use my device as long as I want to.

I responded, but she didn't hear me, so I just smiled and gave her a hug instead.

Welcome Class

3+3
4+2
5+1

Nobody can hear me.

Hmm...I wonder why.

But that's okay.

I'll use my device to talk today!

www.ingramcontent.com/pod-product-compliance
Lightning Source LLC
LaVergne TN
LVHW070839080426
835511LV00025B/3488